OBSERVING NATURE

Spider

Written by Stephen Savage

Illustrated by Phil Weare

Thomson Learning
New York

Ant   Rabbit

Butterfly   Salmon

Duck   Seagull

Frog   Spider

First published in the
United States in 1995 by
Thomson Learning
New York, NY

Published simultaneously in
Great Britain by
Wayland (Publishers) Ltd.

Library of Congress Cataloging-in-
    Publication Data
Savage, Stephen, 1965–
  Spider / written by Stephen Savage ; illustrated
by Phil Weare.
        p.   cm.—(Observing nature)
  Includes index.
  ISBN 1-56847-424-5 (hc)
  1. Aranea diadematus—Juvenile literature.
2. Aranea diadematus—Life cycles—Juvenile
literature. 3. Spiders—Juvenile literature.
[1. Illustrates the life cycle of the garden spider.
2. Spiders.] I. Weare, Phil, ill. II. Title.
III. Series: Savage, Stephen, 1965–   Observing
nature.
QL458.42.A7S37   1995
595.4'4—dc20   95-15394

Printed in Italy

Contents

What Is a Spider?

Spiders come in all shapes, colors, and sizes.

They are not insects, like ants and butterflies,

because they have eight legs rather than six.

Some spiders run along the ground

looking for food, and other spiders

make webs to catch their food.

The type of spider that you are most likely to see is the garden spider. This spider makes a large sticky web to catch flies, grasshoppers, and other flying insects. Although the garden spider has eight eyes, it cannot see very well.

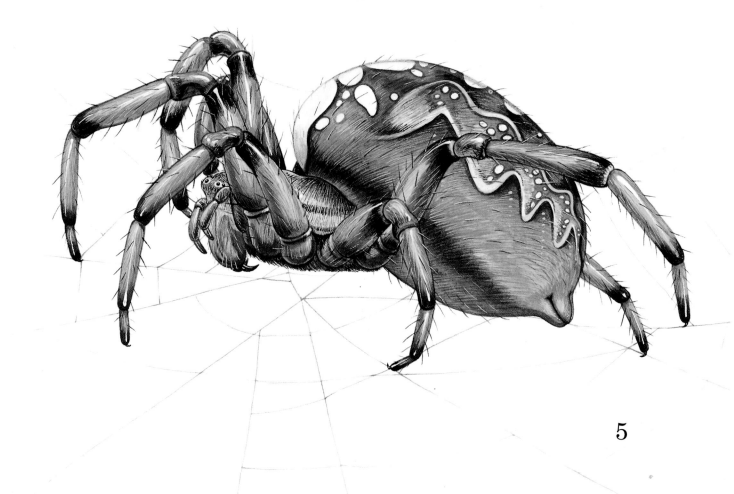

Male and Female

The male and female garden spider look very different.
The female spider is much larger than the male and so
she is easier to spot. It is usually the female that we see
sitting in the center of a web.

6

The male garden spider is smaller and very skinny. You can recognize a garden spider by the pattern of white spots on its body. The white spots are in the shape of a cross.

Making a Web

Spiders make their webs from silk that is made inside their bodies. The spider squeezes the silk out of its body like a thin line of toothpaste. First the spider makes a few lines of the web and sticks them to plants.

The spider then moves
around the web, filling
in the gaps with more
silk threads. This silk is
dry, so the spider will
not get stuck to it.

9

Sticky Web

The spider then moves around and around its web, squeezing out a sticky strand of silk. The sticky silk makes a big circular pattern. This is the part that will catch flying insects. An hour later, the web is finished.

The spider has special feet for walking on its web. It also has oily legs that keep it from getting stuck. The spider is now hungry and waits for an insect to fly into the web.

Catching a Meal

The large fly buzzing around nearby
does not see the spider web.
Suddenly, it flies into the web
and becomes stuck. The fly
struggles, but it
cannot escape.

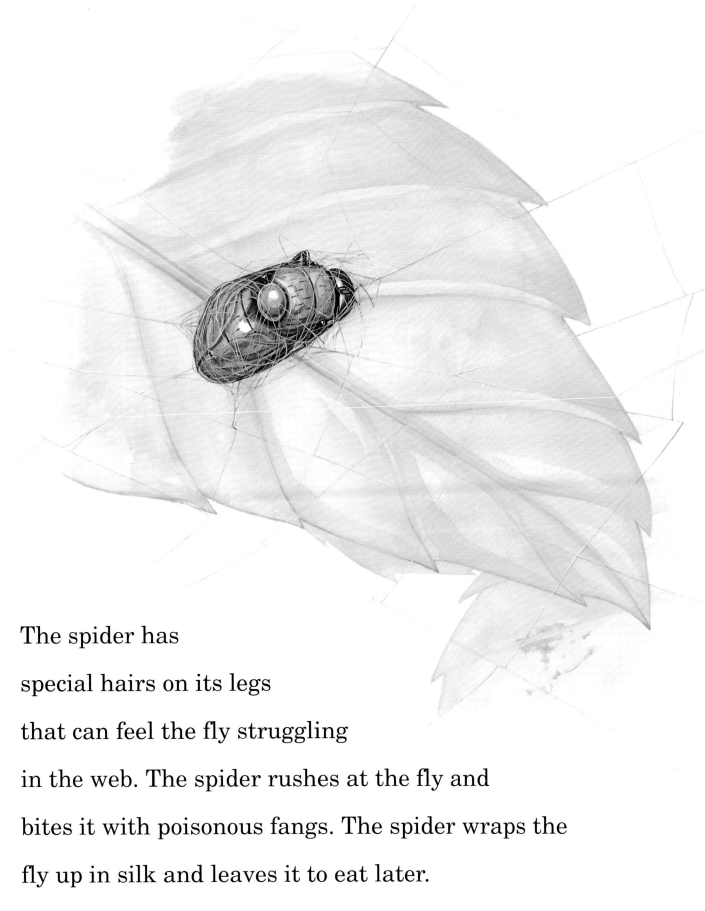

The spider has
special hairs on its legs
that can feel the fly struggling
in the web. The spider rushes at the fly and
bites it with poisonous fangs. The spider wraps the
fly up in silk and leaves it to eat later.

Mating

In August, the male garden spider

goes in search of a female. This is dangerous,

because at this time the female spider is much bigger

than he is. If he is not careful, the female may make

a mistake and eat the male spider.

Once the male has found a female, he taps the web with his legs. If the female rushes out, the male spider must move away and try again. Eventually, the female and male spider mate.

Cocoon Nest

The male spider quickly climbs away and leaves the nest-making to the female. In September, the female spider finds a safe place to spin a silk saucer-shaped nest.

The female spider may
build the nest under some
tree bark or in a bush. She then
lays about 800 eggs. She spins more
yellow silk to cover the eggs. The closed
nest, called an egg sac, protects the eggs from
danger. Soon after this, the female spider dies.

Hatching

It is not until spring that the spider eggs finally hatch. At first, the tiny spiders stay inside the cocoon. The newly hatched spiders have no color and cannot make a web or feed themselves. The baby spiders, called spiderlings, still have some of the egg yolk food inside their bodies.

After a few days, the spiderlings
shed their outer covering, called an
exoskeleton, for the first time. A few days
later, on a warm sunny day, the spiderlings
bite their way out of the cocoon.

Safety in Numbers

The young spiders' white skin has gone. The spiderlings are now a beautiful gold and black. The spiderlings stay together in a large ball-shaped lump for safety. You may see a round ball of baby spiders outdoors.

When danger is near, the tiny
spiderlings run off in different directions.
When the danger has passed, the spiderlings
come out of hiding. They slowly move back into
a ball shape again.

21

Molting

After a few days, the spiderlings go off on their own. You may be surprised one morning to find your garden full of tiny spider webs. In the center of each web is a tiny gold and black spiderling.

molted skin
of spider

The spiderling's body is protected by a hard covering. As the spiderling grows bigger, it has to get rid of its old covering. This is called molting.

23

Dangers

Birds are garden spiders' main enemies. The garden spider has an emergency silk line attached to its body. If the spider is attacked, it can quickly lower itself out of reach from danger.

A garden spider will
molt its outer covering
several times before it
becomes an adult. If a spider
loses a leg to an attacker, it can grow a
new one the next time it molts.

All Grown Up

hover fly

Many of the spiderlings will be attacked
and eaten before they become adults.
This is why the female spider lays
so many eggs. The spiderlings
that survived are now grown
up and will not molt again.

housefly

grasshopper

Soon, the male spiders will go in search of a female. They will mate, and the females will lay eggs that will hatch the following spring.

banded snail

ants

Other Spiders

Here are some other types of spiders that you may see. Hunting spiders, such as the wolf spider, have good eyesight. Instead of making webs, they creep up on their prey.

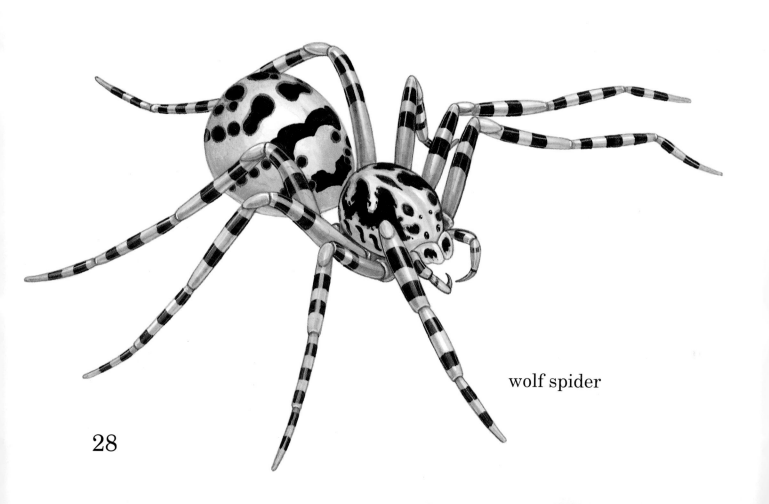

wolf spider

Jumping spiders actually attack insects by leaping on top of them. They also jump from one plant to another as they search for a meal.

zebra jumping spider

spitting spider

Spitting spiders creep up on their prey. Then they trap their meal by spitting out two lines of sticky thread.

Life Cycle of a Spider

1 Male and female

2 Making a web

3 Sticky web

4 Catching a meal

5 Mating

6 Cocoon nest

7 Hatching

8 Safety in numbers

9 Molting

10 Dangers

11 All grown up

Glossary

cocoon A silky covering to protect the spider's eggs.

exoskeleton The hard skin of a spider or insect. These creatures do not have skeletons inside them the way humans do; instead their bodies are supported by the hard exoskeleton.

fangs The long and pointed hollow teeth through which poison is injected into the prey to kill it.

mate When a male and female join together to produce young.

poisonous If something is poisonous it can make the prey sick or cause it to die.

Index